Communication Skills That Every CIO Must Have

Tips And Techniques For CIOs To Use In Order To Become Better Communicators

"Practical, proven techniques that will help you to make your CIO career long and successful"

Dr. Jim Anderson

Published by:
Blue Elephant Consulting
Tampa, Florida

Copyright © 2018 by Dr. Jim Anderson

All rights reserved. No part of this book may be reproduced of transmitted in any form or by any means, electronic or mechanical, including photocopying, recording or by any information storage and retrieval system without written permission of the publisher, except for inclusion of brief quotations in a review.

Printed in the United States of America

Library of Congress Control Number: 2018906126

ISBN-13: 978-1719271387

ISBN-10: 1719271380

Warning – Disclaimer

The purpose of this book is to educate and entertain. This book does not promise or guarantee that anyone following the ideas, tips, suggestions, techniques or strategies will be successful. The author, publisher and distributor(s) shall have neither liability nor responsibility to anyone with respect to any loss or damage caused, or alleged to be caused, directly or indirectly by the information contained in this book.

Other Books By The Author

Product Management

- Developing World Class Products: Techniques For Product Managers To Better Understand What Their Customers Really Want

- Managing Your Product Manager Career: How Product Managers Can Find And Succeed In The Right Job

Public Speaking

- Unforgettable Presentations That Can Change The World: Presentation techniques that will transform a speech into a memorable event

- Creating Speeches That Work: How To Create A Speech That Will Make Your Message Be Remembered Forever!

CIO Skills

- How CIOs Can Bring Business And IT Together: How CIOs Can Use Their Technical Skills To Help Their Company Solve Real-World Business Problems

- New IT Technology Issues Facing CIOs: How CIOs Can Stay On Top Of The Changes In The Technology That

Powers The Company

IT Manager Skills

- How IT Managers Can Use New Technology To Meet Today's IT Challenges: Technologies That IT Managers Can Use In Order to Make Their Teams More Productive

- How To Build High Performance IT Teams: Tips And Techniques That IT Managers Can Use In Order To Develop Productive Teams

Negotiating

- The Art Of Packaging A Negotiation: How To Develop The Skill Of Assembling Potential Trades In Order To Get The Best Possible Outcome

- Getting What You Want In A Negotiation By Learning How To Signal: How To Develop The Skill Of Effective Signaling In A Negotiation In Order To Get The Best Possible Outcome

Miscellaneous

- How To Heal A Broken Leg – Fast!: Understanding how to deal with a broken leg in order to start walking again quickly

- How Software Defined Networking (SDN) Is Going To Change Your World Forever: The Revolution In Network Design And How It Affects

- **Note:** See a complete list of books by Dr. Jim Anderson at the back of this book

Acknowledgements

Any book like this one is the result of years of real-world work experience. In my over 25 years of working for 7 different firms, I have met countless fantastic people and I've been mentored by some truly exceptional ones. Although I've probably forgotten some of the people who made me the person that I am today, here is my attempt to finally give them the recognition that they so truly deserve:

- Thomas P. Anderson
- Art Puett
- Bobbi Marshall
- Bob Boggs

Dr. Jim Anderson

This book is dedicated to my wife Lori. None of this would have been possible without her love and support.

Thanks for the best 21 years of my life (so far)...!

Table Of Contents

CIOS NEED TO HAVE GOOD COMMUNICATION SKILLS 9

ABOUT THE AUTHOR 11

CHAPTER 1: A CIO ALWAYS HAS TO MAINTAIN CREDIBILITY 16

CHAPTER 2: IS TOUGH TALKING THE NEW CORRECT WAY TO COMMUNICATE? 21

CHAPTER 3: WHEN SHOULD A CIO TELL THE WORLD THAT THEY HAVE BEEN HACKED? 25

CHAPTER 4: IS A "WALK AND TALK" THE BEST WAY TO CONNECT WITH YOUR DIRECT REPORTS? 29

CHAPTER 5: HOW A CIO CAN BECOME VERY PERSUASIVE 33

CHAPTER 6: WHAT'S THE BEST WAY FOR A CIO TO COMMUNICATE? 38

CHAPTER 7: WHEN CYBERATTACKED, SHOULD CIOS SHARE INFORMATION ABOUT THE EXPERIENCE? 42

CHAPTER 8: SKILLS THAT EVERY CIO NEEDS TO HAVE 47

CHAPTER 9: IT TURNS OUT THAT CIOS WANT THEIR PRIVACY 52

CHAPTER 10: HOW CAN CIOS TEACH THEIR EMPLOYEES ABOUT CYBERSECURITY? 56

CHAPTER 11: HOW CIOS CAN DO A GOOD JOB OF DELIVERING BAD NEWS 61

CHAPTER 12: CIOS NEED TO LEARN HOW BEST TO USE EMAIL 65

CIOs Need To Have Good Communication Skills

It's great for a CIO to have a good idea, but if it stops there then it's not going to do anyone any good. CIOs need to be able to communicate their thoughts with the rest of their department and the company in order to maintain credibility as a thought leader. How each of us communicates is a personal choice, we have many ways of doing this from tough talking to conversations. The most important point is that we share our information with others.

What to communicate is a critical question that every CIO is going to have to answer for themselves. When the company suffers a digital attack, what needs to be communicated, to whom, and how? When we need to connect with members of our team, is going for a walk with them the right method to get our point across?

Effective communication is a set of skills that every CIO needs to develop. Our goal has to be to make any communication that we do be effective – we want to come across as being persuasive. We need to be able to get our information across when we are talking about critical issues like cybersecurity.

CIOs communicate in a variety of different ways. We have opportunities to share both good news and bad news. We need to know how to do both well. Email is one of the most commonly used communication tools by CIOs. However, we don't always use it well. We need to take the time to make sure that our emails will be opened and that they will cause people to take action.

For more information on what it takes to be a great CIO, check out my blog, The Accidental Successful CIO, at:

www.TheAccidentalSuccessfulCIO.com

Good luck!

- Dr. Jim Anderson

About The Author

I must confess that I never set out to be a CIO. When I went to school, I studied Computer Science and thought that I'd get a nice job programming and that would be that. Well, at least part of that plan worked out!

My first job was working for Boeing on their F/A-18 fighter jet program. I spent my days programming fighter jet software in assembly language and I loved it. The U.S. government decided to save some money and went looking for other countries to sell this plane to. This put me into an unfamiliar role: I started to meet with foreign military officials and I ended up having to manage groups of engineers who were working on international projects.

Time moved on and so did I. I found myself working for Siemens, the big German telecommunications company. They were making phone switches and selling them to the seven U.S. phone companies. The problem was that the switches were too complicated. Customers couldn't tell the difference between one complicated phone switch from another complicated phone switch. Once again I found myself working with the sales and marketing teams to find ways to make the great technology that the engineers had developed understandable to both internal and external customers.

I've spent over 25 years working as a senior IT professional for both big companies and startups. This has given me an opportunity to learn what it takes to manage and IT department in ways that allow it to maximize its output while becoming a valuable part of the overall company.

I now live in Tampa Florida where I spend my time managing my consulting business, Blue Elephant Consulting, teaching college courses at the University of South Florida, and traveling to work with companies like yours to share the knowledge that I have about how to create and manage successful IT departments.

I'm always available to answer questions and I can be reached at:

Dr. Jim Anderson
Blue Elephant Consulting
Email: jim@BlueElephantConsulting.com
Facebook: http://goo.gl/1TVoK
Web: http://www.BlueElephantConsulting.com/

"Unforgettable communication skills that will set your ideas free..."

Create IT Departments That Are Productive And A Valuable Asset To The Rest Of The Company !

Dr. Jim Anderson is available to provide training and coaching on the topics that are the most important to people who have to manage IT departments: how can I build a productive IT department (and keep it together) while at the same time providing the rest of the company with the IT services that they need?

Dr. Anderson believes that in order to both learn and remember what he says, speakers need to laugh. Each one of his speeches is full of fun and humor so that what he says "sticks" with everyone.

Dr. Anderson's CIO SkillsTraining Includes:

4. How to identify and attract the right type of IT workers to your IT department.
5. How to build relationships with the company's senior management in order to get the support that you need?
6. How to stay on top of changing technology and security issues so that you never get surprised?

Dr. Jim Anderson works with over 100 customers per year. To invite Dr. Anderson to work with you, contact him at:

Phone: 813-418-6970 or
Email: jim@BlueElephantConsulting.com

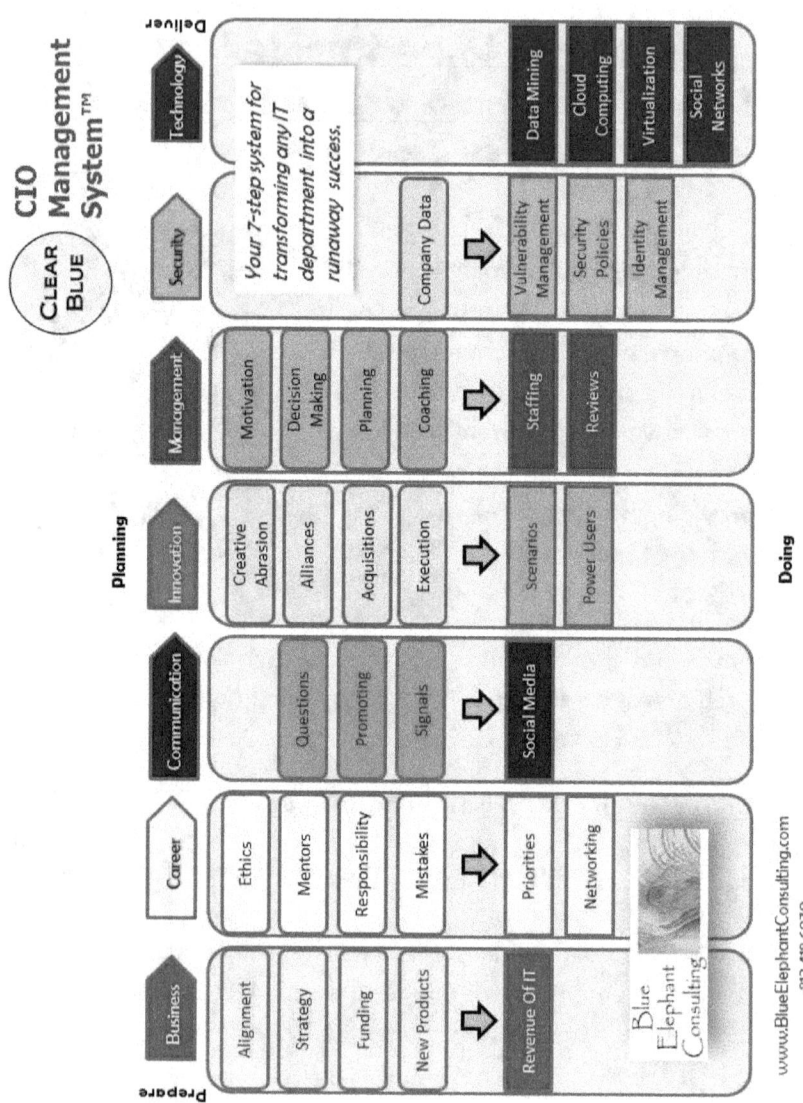

The Clear Blue CIO Management System™ has been created to provide CIOs and senior IT managers with a clear roadmap for how to manage an IT department. This system shows CIOs what needs to be done and in what order to do it.

Chapter 1

A CIO Always Has To Maintain Credibility

CREDIBILITY

Chapter 1: A CIO Always Has To Maintain Credibility

Quick question for you: if I asked someone that you know **if you were a credible person**, what would they tell me? I think that both you and I hope that they would tell me that "yes" you are a credible person. However, if I asked them the same thing about your IT department, what would they say then?

How IT Departments Have Lost Credibility

Over the past few years, there have been a number of very large scale projects that have had the IT department at their very core. When the need for these projects first showed up, the IT department saw the opportunity that they presented and stepped forward to play a leadership role by selling the rest of the company on the importance of information technology. Two such projects come to mind right off the bat: Y2k and ERP projects. The IT department told the rest of the company that these projects were critical to the very survival of the company and it got everyone to support the project. **That's when the problems started to arise**.

The Y2k event (New Year's day back in 2000) came and went and really, nobody had any significant IT related problems – even the firms that had not made the enormous investments in Y2k upgrades that other firms had made. This severely dented ITs credibility. The next major project was the wave of ERP projects that installed a single large program to run the entire company from top to bottom. Almost without fail, these huge projects disrupted the entire company as older applications that everyone was used to using were replaced with new applications that the company's processes may not have been customized for. The end result of all of this change was that the company was thrown into disarray as the new monster program was installed and in the end, **the benefits of switching to the** new ERP way of doing business were never very clearly realized**.

All too often what CIOs forget to tell the rest of the world is that not all of our IT projects are going to be run-way successes. Not every investment in an IT project will result in the company realizing a 10x payback within a short period of time. Just like with any other project that we deal with, **IT projects can experience both setbacks and screw-ups** that cause it to deliver much less than perhaps was originally expected. It's what the person in the CIO position does when this happens that really determines how much credibility they have.

How To Gain Credibility For Your IT Department

Credibility is a funny thing. It can be very hard to get, it can take a long time to get it, and yet it can be so very easy to lose it almost overnight. This is something that many IT departments have discovered when they sold the rest of the company on committing time, energy, funds, and resources to a big IT project that ended up not really having much of a payoff. What the person with the CIO job wants to do when this happens is to run and hide, not talk about the project anymore, and instead talk about the next big thing that IT will be doing. **This is the wrong approach**.

Instead, what you need to do as a CIO is to acknowledge when an IT project goes wrong. You need to make sure that you don't suddenly stop talking about them or delivering status updates on them to the rest of the company. Don't even think about doing something clever with naming such as starting to call the project a "teaching experience" or just say that it has "issues". You especially don't want to try to pin the failure of your IT project on another part of the company. Instead, the correct thing to do is to lay out for all to see what went wrong on this project. Don't run from it, don't hide from it. Instead, **acknowledge what happened and use it as a learning experience for your department.**

CIOs have the job of attempting to communicate to the rest of the company just how important the IT department is and exactly what the IT department can do in order to make the entire company be more competitive. However, it's going to be our credibility that will convince the rest of the company to go along with what we are recommending. **This credibility is a very, very fragile thing**. If we don't take the time to make sure that we are constantly under promising and over delivering then we run the risk of ending up stretching the truth just little bit too far. This is something that our credibility won't be able to recover from.

What All Of This Means For You

CIOs are in charge of the company's IT shop. We do a lot of projects that benefit the company. Sometimes we even uncover an opportunity to do a big project that will fundamentally change how the company works. In order to get support for doing these projects, **the IT department needs to have credibility with the rest of the company** and it turns out that this is a hard thing to get and to keep.

In the past the IT department has told the rest of the company that the sky was falling and that the IT department was the only department that could do anything about it. Two very clear examples of this were the Y2k incident and the arrival of ERP projects. Y2k came and went without the forecasted disaster that the IT department had been warning about. Then ERP projects came and adversely affected the entire company without delivering the promised benefits. **The credibility of the IT department has been damaged and it's going to be up to the CIO to find ways to get it back.**

Credibility is something that you can't see, can't touch, and in many cases can't even describe. However, having it is critical to the successful operation of any IT department. It is the responsibility of the CIO to understand where your IT department stands in terms of credibility and then **to always be taking steps to boost your credibility in the eyes of the rest of company.**

Chapter 2

Is Tough Talking The New Correct Way To Communicate?

Chapter 2: Is Tough Talking The New Correct Way To Communicate?

When you are at the office, how do you interact with people? I suspect that in your office there are smart people, dumb people, nice people, and not so nice people. You probably grin and bear it – you try to treat everyone the same way and **you try to be nice to everyone**. What if you didn't have to do this? At some companies, a radical way of how people interact is being tried out: honesty.

Say Hello To Radical Candor

The first, and perhaps the most important question, is why change anything? The simple reason that some firms are exploring a different way for us to interact is because they believe that the modern office may have become "too nice" even as they have started to realize the importance of information technology. What this means is that because we are so highly aware of what is "politically correct" that **we'll more often than not hold our tongue**. We won't say what we are really feeling. Because of this bad ideas take up a lot of our time and poor managers waste even more of it.

What these firms are asking us to do is to stop being so polite to everyone. Instead, what they want us to do is to drop our workplace veneer. They want us to **start to speak frankly to each other no matter what the situation is**. This approach to workplace communication goes by many names, but two of the most popular are "radical candor" and "front stabbing". I'm pretty sure that you can well imagine that not everyone in the workplace is going to be comfortable with this new way of doing things.

The thinking here is that getting radical candor feedback is going to hurt people's feelings. However, the firms believe that

a bruised ego is going to be better in the long run than the resentment, stalled projects, and low performers that currently exist in our IT departments. As the person with the CIO job, you are going to have to realize that if this is the type of feedback that you want and need from your staff, then you are going to have to show them how to do it – they won't understand otherwise. You are going to have to show people that they need to confront people that they believe are taking the department in the wrong direction or are planning on a project that won't be able to achieve its goals.

How To Give Tough Feedback

If you decide that changing your department so that everyone is not hiding behind a mask of civility and instead is willing to tell everyone else just exactly how they see things, then you are going to have to make some changes. One of the most important things that you are going to have to communicate to your staff is that **they are going to need to have thick skin to work in your IT department** – blunt feedback can hurt feelings. You'll also have to tell people that when they are receiving tough feedback, they'll need to either defend themselves or, if they agree with what they are being told, make some changes.

There are a lot of ways to look at this style of interaction. One positive way is to view it as being **more caring than the traditional way of going behind someone's back when you think that they are doing something wrong**. Radical condor has been defined as giving criticism while showing genuine concern. The thinking is that you wouldn't be giving the feedback if you didn't want the person to improve.

How to give this feedback is the trick. There are a lot of ways of going about doing this. One such way is to offer to **go for a walk with the person that you want to give your feedback to**. Because you'll both be walking in the same direction, your feedback will seem less confrontational. The worst way to provide this feedback is by sitting across the table from each other. This is clearly confrontational and should be avoided at all costs. The thinking is that you need to evaluate the people that you work with accurately, not kindly.

What All Of This Means For You

Good communication is the key to running a successful IT department. People in the CIO position that want to make their departments even better are starting to think about ways that that they can **cut through the veneer of civility** that we all maintain in the modern workplace. What these CIOs want is for their staff to use radical candor to break down walls.

Radical candor consists of **people telling people exactly what they think of their ideas and their management style**. Gone are the attempts to not hurt someone's feelings or to avoid making them feel bad. Instead the idea is that having a bruised ego now is far better than allowing a bad project or a bad idea to move forward in the IT department for any longer than it has to. There are a lot of different ways to communicate this information but the basic idea is to be straightforward while at the same time trying to be as gentle as you can.

This idea has some merits; however, it comes with a lot of risks also. Ultimately it probably comes down to **the type of people that you currently have in your IT department**. Do you think that they could handle having people tell them to their face what they think of both their ideas and themselves? If you think that they could handle it, then perhaps adding radical candor to your IT department is what is needed to move you to the next level.

Chapter 3

When Should A CIO Tell The World That They Have Been Hacked?

Chapter 3: When Should A CIO Tell The World That They Have Been Hacked?

As CIOs we spend a great deal of our time attempting to secure the company's networks from the bad guys because we understand the importance of information technology. This activity takes on a whole host of different forms: firewalls, end user training, security sweeps, etc. However, **sometimes despite our best efforts the bad guys make it over the wall and are able to break into our systems.** We may discover this in a number of different ways: log files of network activity, files that have been tampered with, missing or deleted data, etc. A critical question that every person with the CIO job needs to find an answer to is when this happens, who do we have to tell?

What Do The Rules Say?

One of the biggest issues that people in the CIO position need to deal with in terms of handling a break in is that this **may have legal implications for the company**. The Securities and Exchange Commission (SEC) has said that any event that is "material" (significant enough to influence and investor's decision to buy the company's stock) has to be reported to the SEC.

However, **fewer and fewer CIOs are electing to do this**. There are roughly 9,000 publicly listed companies and since 2010 only 10 of them have told the SEC that they have experienced a cyber break in. This is a problem because is a well-known fact that the number of known break ins across all types of businesses (both public and private) in the U.S. since 2010 totals 2,642.

It's not like CIOs are not trying to prevent these events from happening. Companies are reported to have spent US$86B last year securing their networks. This was up 18% from the year before. This year companies are expected to spend $94B on such efforts. The issue has become so serious that a number of states have implanted laws that **require firms to report cyber break ins** that compromise more than a given set of consumer data such as phone numbers or credit card info.

What Is Being Set Up For Reporting?

Since a break in could have an effect on the company's stock price, these break ins are **starting to get the attention of company boards**. The boards are trying to determine the customer and financial impact of a breech in order to determine if they are required to report it to the SEC. The issue of cyber security is so important that it has become a reoccurring issue that boards will be revisiting throughout the year.

The problem with the SEC reporting system is that there is no clear way to determine if a break in meets the reporting criteria. Firms are very aware that as of yet the SEC has not started a court case against a firm for not reporting a break in; however, the SEC has been very clear that **they could do this at any time**. From an investor point-of-view, they want more information about a company's battles with cyber criminals. They are most interested in events that will impact a company's profits.

The American Institute of CPAs has gone ahead and created new guidelines that CIOs can use in reporting how they are securing their networks against the bad guys. The challenge here for CIOs is that **they really don't want to offer either too little or too much information to the company's investors**. If a CIO does not come clean about a data breech happening, then investors may believe that something is being hidden from them. Alternatively, there are a lot of minor security events that occur each day that if you notified investors about would just create a lot of unnecessary noise. CIOs are going to have to learn how to strike a balance.

What All Of This Means For You

In the world of CIOs there is probably no more important job than finding ways to secure the company's networks. We spend both a great deal of time and money to keep our networks safe. The bad guys may still find a way in and if they do, we need to make a decision about whether or not we tell the world about what just happened.

The Securities and Exchange Commission requires companies to report any "material" events that may influence an investor who might be thinking about buying the company's stock. **CIOs need to determine if a cyber break in fits this definition**. Since 2010, even as break ins have increased, very few CIOs have done this despite spending great deals of money on trying to protect their networks. Company boards are starting to get involved because of the potential impact of these events. Investors are starting to ask for more network security information because they want to know if breeches will impact profits. CIOs are going to have to determine if an event is worth reporting to the public.

The one thing that we know about the future is that CIOs will continue to keep trying to secure their networks and the bad guys will keep trying to break in. There will always be the case where the bad guys **do find a way to get inside of your network** and when this happens you have decisions that have to be made. Make sure that you understand the impact of the break in and then do the right thing!

Chapter 4

Is A "Walk And Talk" The Best Way To Connect With Your Direct Reports?

Chapter 4: Is A "Walk And Talk" The Best Way To Connect With Your Direct Reports?

Think for just a moment about the last meeting that you went to. How did that turn out for you? Can you remember what was said? Even more interestingly, were you any healthier once the meeting was over. I'm willing to bet that the answer was no. Don't you wish that, assuming that these meetings are a necessity, **there was a better way to conduct them?** It turns out that there is. Depending on the size of the meeting that people are having with the person who has the CIO job, a "walk and talk" just might be a better way of communicating with the members of your department.

The Benefits Of A Walk And Talk

So first off, let's make sure that we are all on the same page when it comes to this "walk and talk" thing. The good news is that it is exactly what it sounds like, **you hold a meeting with one or more people while all of you are walking**. Instead of having to have your meeting in any one of the boring conference rooms at your work location, you now have a number of different locations where you can hold your walk and talk meetings: outside, in a park, or even in the halls at your office.

These meeting often take place over a set route – you don't want to have to be distracted trying to figure out where you want to go next. They also generally have a fixed amount of time that they are going to occur in. 30 minutes seems to be the norm. You might think that it could be difficult to get others to join you for a walk and talk meeting; however, you may be surprised. The reasons that people are **willing to meet this way** are varied but they include having a desire to boost their daily step count or people who have been reading the latest research that shows that we all need to become more mobile while we are at work.

As with all workplace activities, the scientists have been hard at work studying the impact of adding walk and talk meetings to your day. What they have found is that people who engage in this type of activity were **less likely to miss work due to health reasons**. By now I think that we all realize that spending the entire day just sitting at our desk can lead to obesity, type 2 diabetes, and lots of other bad health issues.

The Proper Way To Hold A Walk And Talk

So if we can all agree that this walk and talk thing might be a good thing for us to start to participate in, the next question is just exactly how should we go about doing it? The first thing that you are going to have to realize is that this type of meeting can't replace all of the meetings that you hold. Rather, it is a good fit for a subset of your meetings. Walk and talk meetings are ideal **when you want to meet with one person**; however, they can also work if you need to talk with two people. However, that's the limit.

The next thing that you need to realize is that unlike a meeting in which everyone will be sitting around, **there is a very clear time limit to walk and talk meetings**. When you realize that you will be making a physical effort to walk during the entire meeting, you need to realize that both you and the people that you are talking with will become tired as the meeting goes on. This means that you need to call a halt to the meeting before anyone becomes too tired to keep up. A good rule of thumb is 30 minutes.

Finally, and this may be the most important rule of all, **you need to let other people know what you are up to**. The reason for this is because if you go off to a park and go for a walk, if people don't realize that you are engaged in a business meeting then they'll probably just assume that you are goofing off. However, if you inform people what you are up to, you'll get credit for holding the meetings and there is a good chance that they'll leave you alone while you are walking and talking.

What All Of This Means For You

Meetings are a part of the life of the person with the CIO position as we try to communicate the importance of information technology to the rest of the company. They are how we get the status updates that we need in order to make good decisions and they are how we let our direct reports know what we want them to do. However, all too often the meetings that we attend **can be both boring and inefficient**. What we need is a new way to hold meetings that will both benefit ourselves and be more effective.

One such way to hold a meeting is to have a "walk and talk". Quite literally **you go for a walk with one or two other people and while you are walking**, you have the same discussions that you would have had if you were sitting in a meeting room somewhere. The health benefits are clear: you will boost your activity and avoid doing even more of that dangerous sitting around stuff. To make this kind of meeting be successful, you need to do several things. You have to limit the number of people who participate to only one or two. You need to limit the time to no more than 30 minutes. Finally, you need to tell other people what you are doing so they don't think that you are just goofing off.

Meetings are how things get done. However, they don't always work and we have a need to stay healthy. Adding walk and talk meetings to our set of tools can provide us with **yet another way to connect with the people who work in our department** and change things up a bit. The next time you need to talk with someone about a topic, suggest that the two of you go for a walk.

Chapter 5

How A CIO Can Become Very Persuasive

Chapter 5: How A CIO Can Become Very Persuasive

What does it take to be a successful CIO? The answer, of course, is that it takes a lot of different things. Most importantly you need to become good at selling both yourself and the importance of information technology to others. Another way of saying this is that **you need to be good at persuading people**. We're not talking about finding ways to either pressure or manipulate people. Rather you just have a way of getting them to want to do what you need them to do. How can the person with the CIO job boost their ability to be persuasive?

Win Them Over

The first thing that we need to understand about being persuasive is that the people that we'll be talking with are not looking to be wowed by data and reasoning. I know, this is a bit disappointing. However, what they are looking for is **you to be confident**. Studies have shown that speakers who come across as knowing their stuff can win over even the most skeptical people. Your audience will naturally associate confidence with skill.

When you want to get a group of people to agree with the idea that you present to them, you need to not present them with your big idea right off the bat. Instead, you are going to want to present them with **some smaller ideas that you are confident that they will agree to**. Different studies have shown that once you can get agreement on smaller issues, this will have an enduring effect for at least a short period of time. Get your audience to agree with you right off the bat and then when you present your big idea, you'll have a much better chance of them agreeing with you.

Somewhat interestingly, **the rate at which you speak can have an impact on how persuasive you will come across as being**. We generally face two different types of audiences: audiences that agree with what we are telling them and audiences that disagree with what we are telling them. It turns out that if your audience disagrees with you, then you should talk faster. Doing so prevents them from coming up with ideas that go against what you are saying. If your audience agrees with what you are saying, then you need to speak slower. This will allow them to evaluate what you are telling them and will allow them to factor in their own thoughts which should help them to persuade themselves.

Know Your Audience

If you want to persuade a group of people to do what you need them to do, you are going to have to find ways to **get them to believe in you**. What this means is that you are going to have to reveal the authentic you to them. You want to show them that you really care. There are a number of different ways to go about doing this. Interestingly enough, showing that you are frustrated is one of them and including a couple of curse words can clearly show that you have a real sense of urgency in regards to what is being discussed.

If you want to get your audience to agree with you, then you are going to have to take into account **how they like to process information**. We all process information differently and so if you start asking your audience to process what you are telling them in a way that doesn't work for them, they'll push back. You don't want them to reject what you are requesting just because of how it was presented to them. Instead, what you need to do is to make sure that you don't push your audience to agree with you right off the bat if that's not their style. However, don't ask them to think about it if they are quick decision makers.

When we present ideas to an audience, we want them to agree with us. What this means is that all too often, we may end up just presenting the good stuff – ideas that support our position. It turns out that your audience realizes that there are **two sides to each coin** and that no idea is perfect. This means that you can become more persuasive if you present one or more opposing ideas. Take the time to show how you can mitigate or overcome those problems.

What All Of This Means For You

As the person in the CIO position, **you need the help of other people in order to get things done**. This is not always an easy thing to make happen. What's going to have to happen is that you are going to have to find ways to persuade other people both inside and outside of your company to do what you need them to do for you. The trick is discovering what it takes to persuade someone...

The first thing that you need to understand when it comes to persuading someone is that **they are not going to be wowed by logic**. Facts and figures will only take you so far. What they are really looking for is someone who is confident in what they are saying. In order to get them to agree with you, you need to be careful to not ask for the big agreement right off the bat. Instead, get them to agree to several small things first and then present them with your main point. Use your rate of speech to get audiences that both disagree and agree with you to be won over to your proposal. To persuade a group of people, they are going to have to feel that they are dealing with the authentic you and so you'll have to reveal the real you to them. Your idea will require them to consider what you are saying and this means that you're going to have to take into account how they process information. Your idea may be a great idea, but there are other ideas. You need to present both to your audience so that they feel that they have a balanced view of what is being discussed.

Persuasion is a key part of being a CIO. You need support from others in order to accomplish all of the things that the company is counting on you to do. This means that **you are going to have to be able to persuade others to do what you need them to do**. Persuasion can be learned and so spend some time getting good at it and you'll become a more effective CIO.

Chapter 6

What's The Best Way For A CIO To Communicate?

Chapter 6: What's The Best Way For A CIO To Communicate?

When you hold the CIO position, because of the importance of information technology you have a great deal of responsibility. This means that you have to come up with ways to let everyone who works for you know what you want them to accomplish. In a word, **you have to communicate**. As easy as this may sound to do, it turns out that it's actually quite difficult to do well. All too often we'll think that we're doing a good job, but then we'll discover that the people that we've been talking to are confused and don't understand what we need them to do. We need to become better communicators.

The Challenge Of Communicating Well

One of the biggest mistakes that I see CIOs making is that they believe that when they have an opportunity to communicate with a group of their staff, **they need to impress them**. They believe that in some way they need to justify the fact that they are CIO and in order to get everyone to agree that this was a good decision, they are going to have to say some very impressive things. It turns out that they are wrong.

In order to impress a group of IT professionals, CIOs generally like to pull out the complexity card. This means that what they are going to do is to create a speech that is dense with information and contains a lot of **very complicated things**. They believe that by delivering a complicated speech they will be seen as being a very smart person.

What these people in the CIO position are missing is that in reality **complexity does not equal intellect**. These CIOs fear that if they make something too simple, it will show a lack of intelligence on their part. In reality, their failure to simplify what they will be talking about shows a lack of confidence on their part. There is even a name for this: the Too Simple Syndrome.

How A CIO Can Communicate Clearly

If a CIO wants to clearly communicate to members of his or her department, then they have to avoid the **Too Simple Syndrome**, and show confidence in simplicity. This all starts by you deciding to not cover more than three major points when you are talking with a group. Within each of these three groups, limit yourself to providing no more than three pieces of information. If you find it hard to do this, then you need to take the time to better understand what you'll be talking about.

One of the sad facts of life is that when you are talking with a group, **they will not remember everything that you tell them**. You need to realize this going in. This means that from the three main pieces of information that you are going to be providing them with, you need to pick just one of them as your "main point". This is going to be the point that you'll have to clarify the best.

Finally, it is possible to have too much to say. When you are planning out what you'll be saying, you need to boost your credibility by **limiting what you say**. What this means for you is that you are going to have to learn how to be precise with both your words and any arguments that you make. The good news here is that the harder you work to simplify your presentation, the better you will come to understand what you'll be saying.

What All Of This Means For You

CIOs are leaders. This means that we need to **clearly communicate to the team that we lead what we need them to do for us**. This is a challenging task and there are a number of ways to go about doing it incorrectly. We need to learn how to do a good of communicating.

The first thing that we need to realize is that **a lot of CIOs do a bad job of communicating**. In order to make themselves look good, they attempt to use any communication opportunity to make things complicated so that they sound important. What generally happens is that the people that they are talking with end up being confused and walk away not knowing what they should be doing. A much better way to go about communicating with team members is to limit yourself to just three main items. Pick one of these items and make sure that it will be the one that people will remember after you are done. As you review your material, feel free to eliminate material to make what you are saying more precise.

Good communication skills are never easy. However, all CIOs should realize that **this is a skill that can be learned**. Take the time to identify exactly what you want to say and then simplify it and limit your main points to just three. Carefully crafting what you want to say will yield dividends as the people that you talk with start to understand what you want them to do.

Chapter 7

When Cyberattacked, Should CIOs Share Information About The Experience?

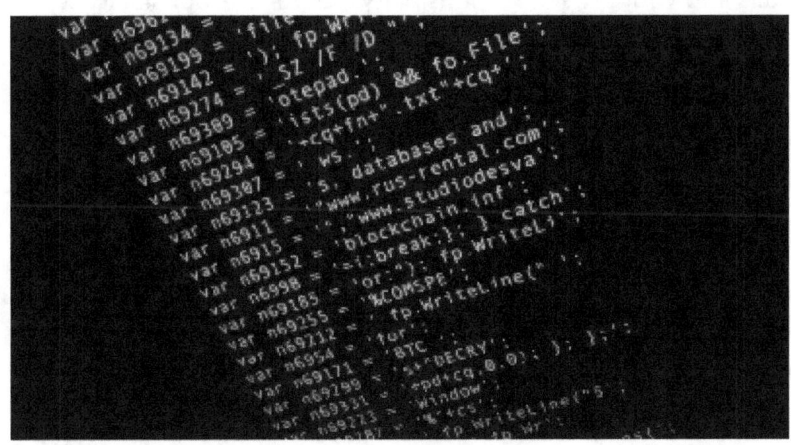

Chapter 7: When Cyberattacked, Should CIOs Share Information About The Experience?

The person with the CIO job, you, is the person who is responsible for securing the company against attacks from outside. We all know that try as we might, we're not going to be able to prevent the bad guys from trying to break into our networks. However, given that we know that they will be coming our way, what kind of obligation do you think that we have to **tell the world when the bad guys do come knocking on our door?** We can keep quiet about it, or we can tell everyone. What's the best thing to do?

What Happens When CIOs Keep Quiet

When you are in the CIO position, you are responsible for knowing everything that is going on in your company's IT department because of the importance of information technology. Any sort of cyber-attack is clearly something that falls into your area of responsibility. Your #1 responsibility will be, of course, **to defend the company against any such attack.** This can be a very dynamic situation and it may require you to call upon many different company IT resources. Additionally, you may also find yourself going to outside firms in order to get the defensive help that you feel that you need.

Once the attack is over and the bad guys have gone away, you then have an important decision to make. You now need to make a decision as to if you are going to be willing to **let the world know that you've come under attack.** One of the key points that you may want to keep in mind is that many other CIOs have chosen to not publically report it when their firms were attacked.

Because of the decision that they have made, what has happened is that other CIOs really don't have a firm grasp of the

scope of the threat that their firms are facing. What it also unfortunately means is that when they are being attacked, CIOs generally don't know the best way to defend their firm. What they are going to do is to end up relying on anecdotal information in order to try to determine what will work against the next wave of cyber-attacks that their firm has to deal with.

The Power Of Sharing Information

Clearly, when it comes to cyber-attacks, having more information puts a CIO into a better position to defend the firm. If a CIO does disclose that his or her firm was hit with a cyber-attack, generally the reason that they are telling the world is because **they were required to by law**. The reason for this is that a cyber-attack that results in the loss of personally identifiable information or medical records are the types that must be publically reported.

It's important for CIOs to realize that the laws regarding mandatory reporting of cyber-attacks **vary by state**. Additionally, the federal regulations differ by industry and are often vague about just exactly what must be reported. The federal government has taken steps to encourage companies to share the information that they have on security breaches. However, there is nothing that currently compels companies to share the information that they have. The end result is that most companies have generic press releases when they are breeched and often don't make any announcement if they suffer from an intrusion.

So what should CIOs be doing? What they should be doing is **reporting each time that they have a cyber incident**. These reports should include both the tactics and the techniques that the hackers used to attempt to get into the company's network. The result of this would be that there would be greater transparency. This knowledge would allow everyone involved to do a better job of understanding how best to handle cyberrisk.

Knowing this would allow decision makers to assess the risks that they are facing in addition to the progress that they are making to defend themselves against these types of risks.

What All Of This Means For You

A CIO is called upon to perform many different tasks. One of the most important of these tasks is **the protection of the company from outsiders who want to do it harm**. One of the biggest questions that we are currently facing is trying to decide just how much we want to share with the rest of the world about our efforts to battle the hackers who are trying to break into our networks.

As you might well guess, it's not the first thought of a CIO to throw open the doors and tell the rest of the world when the company has been hacked. Your initial task is to deal with the attack as it is happening. Once it is over, then you've got decisions to make. Since very few other CIOs report when their firms are attacked, **there is very little information for you to use to determine the scope of the threats that your firm is facing**. Some cyber-attacks do have to be reported by CIOs: the ones where customer information was lost. The reports on these attacks are often generic and don't contain a great deal of information. What CIOs need are complete reports from other CIOs. These reports should contain things like the techniques and tactics used by the hackers. Armed with this information, CIOs would have a better understanding of the types of threats their firms are facing.

CIOs have a difficult decision to make. They need to balance their desire for privacy and the saving of face against **their need to understand the scope of the threats that their firms are facing**. Becoming more transparent about the types of threats that their firm is dealing with can only help other CIOs. If those CIOs choose to do the same thing, then perhaps CIOs will start to be able to sleep better at night knowing that their network is secure.

Chapter 8

Skills That Every CIO Needs To Have

Chapter 8: Skills That Every CIO Needs To Have

Congratulations on having your company make you the CIO. However, now what? As the person with the CIO job, you are going to have to use your skills to solve a range of challenging technical problems. However, you're not going to be able to do this by yourself. **You'll need help from everyone who is a part of your department**. Your big challenge is going to be finding a way to connect with them and motivate them to help you out. Just exactly how are you going to go about doing this?

Being The CIO Is Unglamorous

If you are like most of us, you view having the CIO position as being a significant career accomplishment. In all honesty, you are probably correct. However, if you want to be a successful CIO you are going to have to get over this. Sure, the title is nice and the office that goes along with it is also impressive. However, in order to be successful you are going to have to be able to **convince people to do things for you** and your title is not going to make this happen.

What you are going to have to come to an understanding of is the simple fact that **you can't be the star of the IT department**. Instead, you are going to be the person who takes care of all of the unglamorous tasks. It's going to be your responsibility to take care of the daily tasks that will be required in order to unify the IT department. It's going to be your job to keep the department moving forward even when they've experienced setbacks and their spirts are sagging.

Break The Rules – For A Purpose

In every company there are a set of rules that everyone is expected to follow all of the time. In fact, as the company's CIO one of your jobs is to ensure that the members of your department play by these rules. However, there will come times when your department runs into a problem that they just can't seem to solve. When this happens, they'll come looking for you to step in and lend a helping hand. You are going to have to evaluate the situation and determine if the company's way of doing business **is helping or hurting the IT department**.

As the CIO **you don't always have to play fair**. If the situation calls for it, you may be called on to do what some people would consider to be unsportsmanlike things. When you do this, you'll be testing the limits of the rules that the company has set up. When you are dealing with a tricky business situation, aggressive tactics can be a valuable tool. You just need to remember that you'll have to return to being the nice CIO once the situation has been dealt with.

Use Practical Communication – Not Big Speeches

One of the most important jobs that a CIO has is to **communicate with the rest of the IT team**. There are a number of different ways to go about accomplishing this. One of the most common ones that we CIOs tend to use is what I like to call the "big speech". You know what I'm talking about here: we gather everyone together and then we spend an hour sharing with them why we'll be doing something, or not doing something, or changing how we do something.

It turns out that this may not be the most effective way for us to get our message across. This is good news for those of us who don't believe that we are skilled public speakers. It turns out that a much better way to get your message out to the rest of the department is to get out into your IT department and circulate widely. What you'll want to be doing is spending your time **talking with everyone about what is going on right now**.

What All Of This Means For You

Because of the importance of information technology, every company needs a CIO. When we are placed in that position, we need to find ways that we can be successful. We're not going to be able to be successful by ourselves, instead we are going to have to **rely on the assistance that we can get from the IT department**. However, in order to get that support, we're going to have to develop the skills that are needed in order to connect with the people who work for us.

The first thing that we need to realize is that being a successful CIO is **a very unglamorous job**. We may be thrilled to have the fancy title; however, it turns out that the CIO is not the hero of the IT department. Rather, we are the people who make sure that the little things get taken care of each day, week, and month. We also have to understand that the company has established rules for good reasons. However, when the IT department runs into a problem, it's going to be up to us to find ways to stretch those rules in order to find ways to allow our team to be successful. In order for your IT team to know what you want them to do, you are going to have to tell them. There are a number of different ways that you can go about doing this. The big speech is one way that we do this. However, a much better way is to circulate within your IT department and talk with everyone about what needs to be accomplished right now.

Success as a CIO is something that can only **be accomplished with the help of your entire IT department**. What you need to learn how to do is to connect with your department in a way that will allow everyone to understand what you want them to do and why. Use the three skills that we've discussed to do a better job of showing your team what you need them to do and then sit back and watch as they amaze you with what they are able to accomplish.

Chapter 9

It Turns Out That CIOs Want Their Privacy

Chapter 9: It Turns Out That CIOs Want Their Privacy

What does your office space look like right now? If your company is like roughly 70% of the firms out there, **you have adopted an "open office" format** where the walls and cubes have all been removed. Something else that often goes away at the same time is a private office for the person with the CIO job. This means that you get to sit with the members of your department – side by side working to try to capture the importance of information technology. Back in the day this kind of set up was all the rage, but lately CIOs have been having second thoughts.

What's Wrong With An Open Office

Wait a minute, wasn't it just a few years ago that this whole open office thing was a big deal? There for a while CIOs thought that it would be a good idea to be able to **sit right next to the members of the IT department**. However, what they have discovered is that by the end of the day, both the person in the CIO position and the members of the IT department are thinking that they both need to have their own space. It didn't always used to be this way. Two decades ago, only 64% of offices were configured in the "open-concept" format.

The reason that CIOs were willing to give up their corner office and sit with the members of their department was because it allowed them to project a level of camaraderie with the people who work for them. However, it turns out that perhaps this was not all that good of an idea in the first place. As CIOs and their employees start to sit closer and closer to each other, **both morale and productivity have started to suffer**. Studies that have been made of open-concept offices have revealed that they can improve communication between different parts of the organization. However, at the same time they end up hurting both an employee's motivation and their ability to focus on what they are working on.

The end result of all of this is that employees have started to look for ways to **create privacy in an open-concept office**. There are a number of different ways that they can go about doing this. One thing that they can do is called "conference room squatting" where they move into a conference room and never leave. Additionally, when an open-concept office has "focus booths" they can be taken over by employees who simply need some privacy in order to focus on what they are working on.

How CIOs Are Solving The Privacy Issue

Since you are the CIO, you have a number of different ways that you can go about **getting your privacy back**. One simple thing that you can do is to go ahead and lease an office for you to use. This can prevent your employees from become distracted when you are worried about something and it starts to show on your face. This will give you a change to recharge your batteries in private and then go back out and mix with your employees.

Studies of how CIOs work have revealed that we tend to perform better when **we are in a territory that we know is clearly ours**. One of the big problems with an open office is that if you want to have a meeting with any of the people in your department, everyone else is going to be able to see this meeting happening. No matter what you really want to talk about with them, everyone else is going to be assuming the worse – that person must be in trouble!

You may not have to actually go out and get an office. You might be able to get away with **semi-enclosing a portion of the office with partitions**. This approach or actually having someplace that you can go in order to be alone can be very valuable. As the CIO you are going to have to be careful to communicate to everyone else what you are doing and why you are doing it. You need to let them know that it's really not about privilege or status. You simply need the space in order to do certain types of work.

What All Of This Means For You

The ability of a CIO to be productive has a lot to do with the work environment that they create for themselves and for the IT department. In the past few years, the open-concept floor plan has taken hold where all walls and partitions are removed between CIOs and the rest of the IT department. It turns out that this seating arrangement **comes with some drawbacks**.

Although the open concept seating arrangement has become very popular in the past few years, it turns out that **it has some disadvantages**. It can improve communication between a CIO and the rest of the IT department. However, at the same time it can cause IT workers to lose motivation and become less productive. Employees will often start to look for ways that they can create privacy for themselves. CIOs have the opportunity to lease separate office space, installing partitions, or finding other ways to create private space for themselves. This space is not designed to be a display of privilege but rather to provide the CIO with a place where productive work can be accomplished.

As a CIO we spend a great deal of time thinking about how our company can use IT to achieve its business goals. However, it turns out that the way that we organize how our IT department is laid out can be just as important as any technical decisions that we make. The open concept approach that was so popular a few years ago is falling out of favor as **CIOs discover that they need private space**. Make sure that you have access to the private space that you need in order to be a successful CIO.

Chapter 10

How Can CIOs Teach Their Employees About Cybersecurity?

Chapter 10: How Can CIOs Teach Their Employees About Cybersecurity?

I think that we can all agree that keeping the company's network secure is one of the person with the CIO position's most important tasks because of the importance of information technology. However, no matter how many firewalls we put in place or how effectively we implement two-factor authentication **we still need to understand the weakest link in our security system: our employees**. What this means for a CIO is that we are responsible for training our staff to not make silly security mistakes. How best to go about doing this? We had better come up with a good solution otherwise all of the fancy security tools in the world won't be keeping the bad guys out.

A New Approach To Cybersecurity Training

How does your firm do cybersecurity training today? If your company is like most companies, then what you try to do is to scare your employees into doing the right things. Most companies have policies that state that they will punish employees who make security mistakes. What happens when there are polices like this is that **all of a sudden security training becomes a big turnoff for employees**. Most of the training that we provide to our employees covers things like trying to teach them to not click on suspicious links that they may receive or making the mistake of using a weak password. It turns out that this type of training doesn't work – employees still end up making security mistakes.

This is the reason that a number of companies are now changing how they approach cyberscurity training. The person with the CIO job is trying all sorts of creative things such as **contests and prizes** as a novel way to teach employees about how to stay safe when they are online. For CIOs who are not comfortable doing things like this, there are other approaches that allow them to rethink their training courses in order to find ways that will allow the students to become more comfortable interacting with the course instructor. Initial feedback seems to indicate that these types of changes are working.

The reason that CIOs are willing to take a look at how their firms are delivering cyberscurity training (and make changes) is because **the largest threat that their firm is currently facing comes from within**. The careless employee is the hackers' easiest way to gain access to the company's network. CIOs have been trying to teach the company's employees the correct ways to act when online; however, studies show that 91% of cyberattacks begin with a so-called "phishing" email in which the hacker gets an employee to click on a link that will provide the hacker with access to the company's network.

Getting The Word Out

The CIO's goal is to get the employees who are taking the cybersecurity training class to **pay attention and learn what they need to be doing**. One unique way that they are trying to make this happen is to take the time to train employees who don't have a security background to deliver the cybersecurity classes. These new trainers are then rewarded with incentives to help out their coworkers by delivering training classes, hosting contests, and basically getting the word out about cybersecurity in a way that is both nontechnical and nonthreatening. The instructors are rewarded with points that can be turned into cash or used to get things that they desire at work such as a special parking spot.

The problem that CIOs are facing is that most of our companies are currently using such things as cybersecurity awareness tests and off-the-shelf tutorials. These simply don't work. The reason that they don't work is because employees see them as a chore and **don't pay attention**. Unfortunately, no matter how much time, energy, and effort is spent trying to warn employees about even simple security measures, our efforts often fail. In a now classic experiment, in 2015 a security company dropped 200 USB sticks in airports and coffee shops around the U.S. What they discovered is that a significant number of people who found the USB sticks picked them up and plugged them into a computer not stopping to think if they could be infected with malware.

The good news in all of this is that studies have shown that when games and other incentives are used to teach proper cybersecurity behavior, they do make an impact. Employees have been shown to **change their behavior** after they engaged in a phishing exercise that sent them encouraging emails when they did something right and reprimanding emails when they did something wrong. It turns out that feedback and behavioral reinforcement messaging was found to lead to improvements in risky cybersecurity behavior. CIOs have discovered that if they can use gaming methodology to deliver their cyberscurity training then they can make it competitive between students in the class. No matter how they do it, CIOs need to find ways to make their cybersecurity training effective!

What All Of This Means For You

CIOs are responsible for making sure that the company's networks are secure. In order to make this happen, we invest in a lot of sophisticated hardware and software in order to both detect and deter the bad guys. However, it turns out that **our greatest network security threat comes from the inside – our own employees**. This means that the CIO needs to come up with an effective way to deliver cybersecurity training.

Traditionally, companies have delivered their cybersecurity training in a way that was designed to scare their employees into not making security mistakes. However, studies have shown that **this type of training is not effective**. A much more effective method appears to be to make the training more fun by using contests and prizes for students. This type of motivation appears to do a better job of communicating the information that CIOs want the cybersecurity course students to learn. Another approach that is being used is to train employees with no security background to deliver the cybersecurity courses. This allows the material to be delivered in a non-threating, non-technical way. Many companies are still trying to use off-the-shelf courses to deliver their cybersecurity training. This has been shown to not work. A better approach is to use games and incentives to get this important information across.

The only way that the company's network is ever going to be really secured is when each and every employee **understands their important role in making this happen**. The CIO has the responsibility to create and deliver cybersecurity training that will allow this to happen. If we take the time to study what kinds of training work the best, then we can create training that will work at our company.

Chapter 11

How CIOs Can Do A Good Job Of Delivering Bad News

Chapter 11: How CIOs Can Do A Good Job Of Delivering Bad News

Let's face it, as CIOs we'd all like to be liked. We enjoy the parts of our job that are fun and which have to do with the importance of information technology. It makes us happy when another large IT project is successfully rolled out. However, life is life and **part of our job is that when there is bad news to be delivered**, we're the ones who have the job to share the news with the people who work for us. Nothing that I can tell you will ever make this an easy thing to do. However, it turns out that there are ways that you can deliver information like this in ways that turn out to be less stressful for you and, perhaps, just a little bit more comforting for the people that you have to deliver it to.

How Not To Deliver Bad News

When it comes to delivering bad news, none of us really want to do this. When the time comes for us to sit down with the people who work for us and deliver some bad news to them, all too often **we'll attempt to find ways to avoid doing this**. One of the more common ways is to simply put it off. Perhaps we're hoping the bad news will go away and we'll never have to share it. That rarely, if ever, happens and so delaying the inevitable is never a good idea.

There are some CIOs who realize that if they allow themselves to feel what their workers are feeling they are going to end up feeling bad. In order to prevent themselves from feeling this way, what they do is to **distance themselves from the people that they are talking with**. The reason that they are doing this is to attempt to shield themselves from the fallout of the bad news that they are delivering.

If this is how you deliver bad news, don't feel too bad about it. Roughly half of the people with the CIO job deliver bad news this way. What we are trying to do when we do this is to not think about both the personal and the potential family consequences of the news that we are delivering. This approach may seem like the easiest path to take at the time; however, studies have shown that **it yields the poorest results**.

How To Deliver Bad News

This bad news stuff is hard to deliver and so now it turns out that there are incorrect ways to deliver it. Great. What's a CIO to do? It turns out that there is a correct way to deliver bad news. What this calls for is the person in the CIO position to **connect with the people that they are delivering the news to**. This means that you need to get involved in the conversation and you need to let your own emotions enter into the conversation.

What is going to happen when you do this is that you are going to be able to handle the conversation more personally. You will also be able to offer more practical guidance to the people that you are talking with about how to deal with the news that you are sharing with them. Showing empathy to people as we share bad news with them is not something that comes easily to most of us. The good news here is that **empathy is something that can be learned**. If we can learn how to be empathetic then our own levels of distress when delivering bad news can go down and we'll be able to do a better job of handling things like conflicts.

When you are having a discussion that involves bad news with someone, you are going to want to **focus on fairness**. Since you are the person who is in charge, you are going to want to show fairness to the people that you are talking with by making your decisions neutrally, explaining your actions, and providing the people that you are talking with a chance to be heard. Note that all of these efforts on your part can help your company out. When you show compassion when delivering bad news the people that you are talking with are less likely to feel aggravated and the "survivors" are committed to the company as everyone moves forward.

What All Of This Means For You

In a perfect world there would be no bad news. As CIOs, we could go into work every day just expecting to have an opportunity to share more good news with everyone who works for us. However, we have to live in the real world and so that means that there both is bad news and **we are the ones who are called on to deliver it to the people who work for us**. How we deliver it is key to our ability to do this successfully.

What we don't want to do is to deliver bad news incorrectly. One way to do this task incorrectly would be to distance ourselves from the people that we are talking with. We might do this to shield ourselves from the effects of our words, but that would be a mistake. A better approach would be to show empathy for the people that we are talking with and let your emotions enter into the conversation. Not all of us know how to show empathy and so the good news is that this can be learned. We need to remember to **show fairness** during these discussion and allow the people that we are talking with to express their thoughts and feelings.

Bad news is something that most of us would rather run and hide from. However, since it is a part of real life, we need to make sure that we know how to deal with it. Connecting with the people that we are delivering the bad news to is the key to being able to do this in a compassionate way. You'll never like delivering bad news, but **with a little bit of practice you can get good at it.**

Chapter 12

CIOs Need To Learn How Best To Use Email

Chapter 12: CIOs Need To Learn How Best To Use Email

Ah, email. What a powerful tool. What an utter nightmare! The person who has the CIO job probably uses email so often that they no longer really spend that much time thinking about it. However, that may be a mistake. What we forget is that email is a tool and if we can learn how best to use it, then **we can become more effective**. The good news is that email is something that the researchers have been spending a lot of time taking a look at. Their goal has been to find out how we can become smarter about how we use email at work in order to boost the importance of information technology. Let's take a look at what their research has uncovered.

When To Respond To Email

One of the classic questions that everyone has always been trying to answer has to do with when is the right time to respond to an email – immediately or later on? The researches discovered that at companies where quickly responding to emails was a prized activity, the workers ended up feeling more stressed, were less productive, were more reactive, and were found to spend less time thinking strategically. One of the reasons that we respond quickly to emails is because we believe that by doing so we'll be able to build strong relationships. However, it turns out that this does not happen.

Another big question that comes along with responding to emails is **if we should deal with our email after work hours**. The person in the CIO position may be tempted to leave their email until they get home and then just sit down and try to power through it. However, it turns out that the people that we are sending these after hours emails to are going to end up feeling more pressure to respond. If they do respond to your email, they are not going to be more efficient. All that they will do is generate more email while at the same time not getting more work done.

When To Send An Email

So why do we send emails? **Our goal is to get the people to whom we are sending our emails to actually read them and then take action based on what they have read.** It is not completely their fault that they may ignore our email – they may have other tasks that are clamoring for their attention. The term for what the people that you are sending emails to are experiencing is called "cognitive overload". This means that their brains are being faced with trying to absorb too much information.

When people are dealing with a page full of email that they now have to read, studies have shown that people will focus on what is on the top of the screen. What this means for you is that if you want to get your email read, you really want to try to **time when you send your email to match up with the time that you think the person that you'll be sending the email to will be checking their email**. It turns out that people reply to email more quickly early in the week and their responses were longer. Additionally, people respond more quickly to emails received between 8am and noon.

How To Negotiate Using Email

Negotiating via email is very hard to do well. The reason that this can be such a challenge is because the experts refer to **email as being a "lean medium"**. What they mean by this is that when we are talking with people face-to-face the other person has a lot of non-verbal cues that they can use to determine what we are really thinking. If we are negotiating over the phone, our tone of voice will communicate how we are really feeling. The problem with negotiating via email is that none of these communication tools are available.

Based on the limited amount of communication channels available, you would think that negotiating via email would be a bad decision, right? That's not necessarily correct. It turns out that there are strengths associated with using email to communicate negotiations. Email gave both parties the opportunity to **rehearse what they wanted to say**. They could also use email to communicate a great deal of information in a clear form that people were able to refer back to at a later date. Email also helped to eliminate common negotiation misunderstandings including missed emails and time-zone problems. It turns out that if you know how to use it correctly, email can be very helpful when it comes to negotiations.

What All Of This Means For You

Email is something that we all use every day. In fact, we use email so much that there is a very good chance that we really don't spend a lot of time thinking about it anymore. However, as CIOs since communication is such a critical part of our job, we really do need to make sure that **we are using email as effectively as possible**. In order to do this, we need to take a careful look at what researchers have been able to find out about how we can make our email more effective.

One of the fundamental questions that we've always been trying to answer is when should we respond to an email. Should we dash off a response the moment the email shows up or should we take our time and send a response later on? Researchers have found that in an environment in which people are quickly replying to emails, **the workers are more stressed and less productive**. Additionally, replying to emails after hours can cause the people that we are writing to start to feel under pressure to respond to us right then. The best time to send an email has been found to be early in the week and early in the day. You'll get a quicker response with more content. Negotiating via email is difficult to do because so many communication channels will not be present. However, if done correctly this form of negotiation can eliminate some of the common negotiating problems.

Email is a major part of our lives right now and it will probably always be a part of our lives. In order to get the most out of this tool, we need to slow down and **take a close look at it**. There are right ways and wrong ways to go about using emails. If we listen to what the researchers are telling us, then we can maximize the benefit of this powerful tool.

It's from the forge of failure that the steel of success is formed.

Hard Work Does Not Guarantee Success, But Success Does Not Happen Without Hard Work.

- Dr. Jim Anderson

Create IT Departments That Are Productive And A Valuable Asset To The Rest Of The Company !

Dr. Jim Anderson is available to provide training and coaching on the topics that are the most important to people who have to manage IT departments: how can I build a productive IT department (and keep it together) while at the same time providing the rest of the company with the IT services that they need?

Dr. Anderson believes that in order to both learn and remember what he says, speakers need to laugh. Each one of his speeches is full of fun and humor so that what he says "sticks" with everyone.

Dr. Anderson's CIO SkillsTraining Includes:

4. How to identify and attract the right type of IT workers to your IT department.
5. How to build relationships with the company's senior management in order to get the support that you need?
6. How to stay on top of changing technology and security issues so that you never get surprised?

Dr. Jim Anderson works with over 100 customers per year. To invite Dr. Anderson to work with you, contact him at:

Phone: 813-418-6970 or
Email: jim@BlueElephantConsulting.com

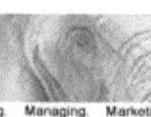

Photo Credits:

Cover - Queen's University
https://www.flickr.com/photos/queensucanada/

Chapter 1: Ron Mader
https://www.flickr.com/photos/planeta/

Chapter 2: Third Way Think Tank
https://www.flickr.com/photos/thirdwaythinktank/

Chapter 3: Matt Joyce
https://www.flickr.com/photos/openfly/

Chapter 4: Lets Go Out Bournemouth and Poole
https://www.flickr.com/photos/letsgoout-bournemouthandpoole/

Chapter 5: Eric
https://www.flickr.com/photos/alendrathril/

Chapter 6: afilimona
https://www.flickr.com/photos/28549876@N02/

Chapter 7: Christiaan Colen
https://www.flickr.com/photos/christiaancolen/

Chapter 8: Robert Stinnett
https://www.flickr.com/photos/rstinnett/

Chapter 9: KylaBorg
https://www.flickr.com/photos/kylaborg/

Chapter 10: Richard Patterson
https://www.flickr.com/photos/136770128@N07/

Chapter 11: Thomas8047
https://www.flickr.com/photos/93482748@N02/

Chapter 12: Jason Markow
https://www.flickr.com/photos/47102677@N04/

Other Books By The Author

Product Management

- Developing World Class Products: Techniques For Product Managers To Better Understand What Their Customers Really Want

- How Product Managers Can Sell More Of Their Product: Tips & Techniques For Product Managers To Better Understand How To Sell Their Product

- How Product Managers Can Sell More Of Their Product: Tips & Techniques For Product Managers To Better Understand How To Sell Their Product

- How To Create A Successful Product That Customers Will Want: Techniques For Product Managers To Boost Product Sales And Increase Customer Satisfaction

- What Product Managers Need To Know About World-Class Product Development: How Product Managers Can Create Successful Products

- How Product Managers Can Learn To Understand Their Customers: Techniques For Product

Managers To Better Understand What Their Customers Really Want

- Product Management Secrets: Techniques For Product Managers To Boost Product Sales And Increase Customer Satisfaction

- Product Development Lessons For Product Managers: How Product Managers Can Create Successful Products

- Customer Lessons For Product Managers: Techniques For Product Managers To Better Understand What Their Customers Really Want

- Product Failure Lessons For Product Managers: Examples Of Products That Have Failed For Product Managers To Learn From

- Communication Skills For Product Managers: The Communication Skills That Product Managers Need To Know How To Use In Order To Have A Successful Product

- How To Have A Successful Product Manager Career: The Things That You Need To Be Doing TODAY In Order To Have A Successful Product Manager Career

- Product Manager Product Success: How to keep your product on track and make it become a success

Public Speaking

- Unforgettable Presentations That Can Change The World: Presentation techniques that will transform a speech into a memorable event

- Creating Speeches That Work: How To Create A Speech That Will Make Your Message Be Remembered Forever!

- How To Organize A Speech In Order To Make Your Point: How to put together a speech that will capture and hold your audience's attention

- Changing How You Speak To Overcome Your Fear Of Speaking: Change techniques that will transform a speech into a memorable event

- Delivering Excellence: How To Give Presentations That Make A Difference: Presentation techniques that will transform a speech into a memorable event

- Tools Speakers Need In Order To Give The Perfect Speech: What tools to use to create your next speech so that your message will be remembered forever!

- How To Create A Speech That Will Be Remembered

- Secrets To Organizing A Speech For Maximum Impact: How to put together a speech that will capture and hold your audience's attention

- How To Become A Better Speaker By Changing How You Speak: Change techniques that will transform a speech into a memorable event

- How To Give A Great Presentation: Presentation techniques that will transform a speech into a memorable event

- How To Rehearse In Order To Give The Perfect Speech: How to effectively rehearse your next speech to that your message be remembered forever!

- Secrets To Creating The Perfect Speech: How to create a speech that will make your message be remembered forever!

- Secrets To Organizing The Perfect Speech: How to organize the best speech of your life!

- Secrets To Planning The Perfect Speech: How to plan to give the best speech of your life

- How To Show What You Mean During A Presentation: How to use visual techniques to transform a speech into a memorable event

CIO Skills

- How CIOs Can Bring Business And IT Together: How CIOs Can Use Their Technical Skills To Help Their Company Solve Real-World Business Problems

- New IT Technology Issues Facing CIOs: How CIOs Can Stay On Top Of The Changes In The Technology That Powers The Company

- Keeping The Barbarians Out: How CIOs Can Secure Their Department and Company: Tips And Techniques For CIOs To Use In Order To Secure Both Their IT Department And Their Company

- What CIOs Need To Know In Order To Successfully Manage An IT Department: Decision Making Skills That Every CIO Needs To Have In Order To Be Able To Make The Right Choices

- Becoming A Powerful And Effective Leader: Tips And Techniques That IT Managers Can Use In Order To Develop Leadership Skills

- CIO Secrets For Growing Innovation: Tips And Techniques For CIOs To Use In Order To Make Innovation Happen In Their IT Department

- Your Success As A CIO Depends On How Well You Communicate: Tips And Techniques For CIOs To

Use In Order To Become Better Communicators

- What CIOs Need To Know About Working With Partners: Techniques For CIOs To Use In Order To Be Able To Successfully Work With Partners

- Critical CIO Management Skills: Decision Making Skills That Every CIO Needs To Have In Order To Be Able To Make The Right Choices

- How CIOs Can Make Innovation Happen: Tips And Techniques For CIOs To Use In Order To Make Innovation Happen In Their IT Department

- CIO Communication Skills Secrets: Tips And Techniques For CIOs To Use In Order To Become Better Communicators

- Managing Your CIO Career: Steps That CIOs Have To Take In Order To Have A Long And Successful Career

- CIO Business Skills: How CIOs can work effectively with the rest of the company!

IT Manager Skills

- How IT Managers Can Use New Technology To Meet Today's IT Challenges: Technologies That IT Managers Can Use In Order to Make Their Teams

More Productive

- How To Build High Performance IT Teams: Tips And Techniques That IT Managers Can Use In Order To Develop Productive Teams

- Save Yourself, Save Your Job – How To Manage Your IT Career: Secrets That IT Managers Can Use In Order To Have A Successful Career

- Growing Your CIO Career: How CIOs Can Work With The Entire Company In Order To Be Successful

- How IT Managers Can Make Innovation Happen: Tips And Techniques For IT Managers To Use In Order To Make Innovation Happen In Their Teams

- Staffing Skills IT Managers Must Have: Tips And Techniques That IT Managers Can Use In Order To Correctly Staff Their Teams

- Secrets Of Effective Leadership For IT Managers: Tips And Techniques That IT Managers Can Use In Order To Develop Leadership Skills

- IT Manager Career Secrets: Tips And Techniques That IT Managers Can Use In Order To Have A Successful Career

- IT Manager Budgeting Skills: How IT Managers Can Request, Manage, Use, And Track Their Funding

- Secrets Of Managing Budgets: What IT Managers Need To Know In Order To Understand How Their Company Uses Money

Negotiating

- The Art Of Packaging A Negotiation: How To Develop The Skill Of Assembling Potential Trades In Order To Get The Best Possible Outcome

- Getting What You Want In A Negotiation By Learning How To Signal: How To Develop The Skill Of Effective Signaling In A Negotiation In Order To Get The Best Possible Outcome

- Exploring How To Get The Deal That You Want In A Negotiation: How To Develop The Skill Of Exploring What Is Possible In A Negotiation In Order To Reach The Best Possible Deal

- Use The Power Of Arguing To Win Your Next Negotiation: How To Develop The Skill Of Effective Arguing In A Negotiation In Order To Get The Best Possible Outcome

- Learn How To Signal In Your Next Negotiation: How To Develop The Skill Of Effective Signaling In A

Negotiation In Order To Get The Best Possible Outcome

- Learn The Skill Of Exploring In A Negotiation: How To Develop The Skill Of Exploring What Is Possible In A Negotiation In Order To Reach The Best Possible Deal

- Learn How To Argue In Your Next Negotiation: How To Develop The Skill Of Effective Arguing In A Negotiation In Order To Get The Best Possible Outcome|

- How To Open Your Next Negotiation: How To Start A Negotiation In Order To Get The Best Possible Outcome

- Preparing For Your Next Negotiation: What You Need To Do BEFORE A Negotiation Starts In Order To Get The Best Possible Deal

- Learn How To Package Trades In Your Next Negotiation

- All Good Things Come To An End: How To Close A Negotiation - How To Develop The Skill Of Closing In Order To Get The Best Possible Outcome From A Negotiation

- Take No Prisoners In Your Next Negotiation: How To Start A Negotiation In Order To Get The Best Possible Outcome

Miscellaneous

- How To Heal A Broken Leg – Fast!: Understanding how to deal with a broken leg in order to start walking again quickly

- How Software Defined Networking (SDN) Is Going To Change Your World Forever: The Revolution In Network Design And How It Affects You

- The Power Of Virtualization: How It Affects Memory, Servers, and Storage: The Revolution In Creating Virtual Devices And How It Affects You

- The Internet-Enabled Successful School District Superintendent: How To Use The Internet To Boost Parental Involvement In Your Schools

- Power Distribution Unit (PDU) Secrets: What Everyone Who Works In A Data Center Needs To Know!

- Making The Jump: How To Land Your Dream Job When You Get Out Of College!

- How To Use The Internet To Create Successful Students And Involved Parents

Your Success As A CIO Depends On How Well You Communicate

This book has been written with one goal in mind – to show you how you can become a CIO who communicates clearly. It's not easy being a CIO so we're going to show you what you need to be doing in order to sure that everyone understands what needs to be done!

Let's Make Your CIO Career A Success!

What You'll Find Inside:

- **A CIO ALWAYS HAS TO MAINTAIN CREDIBILITY**
- **WHEN CYBERATTACKED, SHOULD CIOS SHARE INFORMATION ABOUT THE EXPERIENCE?**
- **HOW CAN CIOS TEACH THEIR EMPLOYEES ABOUT CYBERSECURITY?**
- **CIOS NEED TO LEARN HOW BEST TO USE EMAIL**

Dr. Jim Anderson brings his 25 years of real-world experience to this book. He's been a senior IT executive at some of the world's largest firms. He's going to show you what you need to do (and not do!) in order to make your CIO career a success!

www.ingramcontent.com/pod-product-compliance
Lightning Source LLC
Chambersburg PA
CBHW052336220526
45472CB00001B/448